FRANCIS FRITH'S

HAVERFORDWEST TOWN AND CITY MEMORIES

THE FRANCIS FRITH COLLECTION

www.francisfrith.com

FRANCIS FRITH'S
TOWN & CITY
MEMORIES

HAVERFORDWEST

TONY CORNISH is married with three children. He has been writing for eighteen years on a variety of subjects and has been published by Oxford University Press and Prentice Hall, among others. He is also the author of the Francis Frith Collection books on the City of Swansea and Wiltshire. As well as book writing he also writes songs and has two albums on release, and is currently studying for an MA in Creative and Critical Writing.

JAMES K PLANT is also married with three children. He is a history graduate and a specialist in 18th and 19th century Welsh history. He is the co-author with Tony Cornish of several other titles for The Francis Frith Collection, including *Llandudno*, *Aberystwyth* and *Rhyl*.

FRANCIS FRITH'S
TOWN & CITY
MEMORIES

HAVERFORDWEST

TONY CORNISH & JAMES K PLANT

First published as Haverfordwest, A Photographic History of your Town
in 2001 by Black Horse Books, an imprint of The Francis Frith Collection
Revised edition published in paperback in the United Kingdom in 2006 by
The Francis Frith Collection as Haverfordwest, Town and City Memories
Paperback Edition ISBN 1-84589-139-2

British Library Cataloguing in Publication Data

Haverfordwest
Town and City Memories
Tony Cornish & James K Plant

The Francis Frith Collection®
Frith's Barn, Teffont,
Salisbury, Wiltshire SP3 5QP
Tel: +44 (0) 1722 716 376
Email: info@francisfrith.co.uk
www.francisfrith.com

Aerial photographs reproduced under licence from Simmons Aerofilms Limited
Historical Ordnance Survey maps reproduced under licence from Homecheck.co.uk

Printed and bound in England

Front Cover: **HAVERFORDWEST, HIGH STREET c1950** H41017t
The colour-tinting in this image is for illustrative purposes only,
and is not intended to be historically accurate

Every attempt has been made to contact copyright holders of illustrative material.
We will be happy to give full acknowledgement in future editions for any items not credited.
Any information should be directed to The Francis Frith Collection.

AS WITH ANY HISTORICAL DATABASE, THE FRANCIS FRITH ARCHIVE IS CONSTANTLY BEING
CORRECTED AND IMPROVED, AND THE PUBLISHERS WOULD WELCOME INFORMATION ON
OMISSIONS OR INACCURACIES

FRANCIS FRITH'S
TOWN & CITY
MEMORIES

CONTENTS

FRANCIS FRITH, Victorian founder of the world-famous photographic archive, was a devout Quaker and a highly successful Victorian businessman. By 1860 he was already a multi-millionaire, having established and sold a wholesale grocery business in Liverpool. He had also made a series of pioneering photographic journeys to the Nile region. The images he returned with were the talk of London. An eminent modern historian has likened their impact on the population of the time to that on our own generation of the first photographs taken on the surface of the moon.

Frith had a passion for landscape, and was as equally inspired by the countryside of Britain as he was by the desert regions of the Nile. He resolved to set out on a new career and to use his skills with a camera. He established a business in Reigate as a specialist publisher of topographical photographs.

Frith lived in an era of immense and sometimes violent change. For the poor in the early part of Victoria's reign work was a drudge and the hours long, and ordinary people had precious little free time. Most had not travelled far beyond the boundaries of their own town or village. Mass tourism was in its infancy during the 1860s, but during the next decade the railway network and the establishment of Bank Holidays and half-Saturdays gradually made it possible for the working man and his family to enjoy holidays and to see a little more of the world. With characteristic business acumen, Francis Frith foresaw that these new tourists would enjoy having souvenirs to commemorate their days out. He began selling photo-souvenirs of seaside resorts and beauty spots, which the Victorian public pasted into treasured family albums.

Frith's aim was to photograph every town and village in Britain. For the next thirty years he travelled the country by train and by pony and trap, producing fine photographs of seaside resorts and beauty spots that were keenly bought by millions of Victorians.

THE RISE OF FRITH & CO

Each photograph was taken with tourism in mind, the small team of Frith photographers concentrating on busy shopping streets, beaches, seafronts, picturesque lanes and villages. They also photographed buildings: the Victorian and Edwardian eras were times of huge building activity, and town halls, libraries, post offices, schools and technical colleges were springing up all over the country. They were invariably celebrated by a proud Victorian public, and photo souvenirs – visual records – published by F Frith & Co were sold in their hundreds of thousands. In addition, many new commercial buildings such as hotels, inns and pubs were photographed, often because their owners specifically commissioned Frith postcards or prints of them for re-sale or for publicity purposes.

In order to gain some understanding of the scale of Frith's business one only has to look at the catalogue issued by Frith & Co in 1886: it runs to some 670 pages. By 1890 Frith had created the greatest specialist photographic publishing company in the world, with over 2,000 stockists! The picture on the right shows the Frith & Co display board on the wall of the stockist at Ingleton in the Yorkshire Dales (left of window). Beautifully constructed with a mahogany frame and gilt inserts, it displayed a dozen scenes.

POSTCARD BONANZA

The ever-popular holiday postcard we know today took many years to appear, and F Frith & Co was in the vanguard of its development. Postcards became a hugely popular means of communication and sold in their millions. Frith's company took full advantage of this boom and soon became the major publisher of photographic view postcards.

Francis Frith died in 1898 at his villa in Cannes, his great project still growing. His sons Eustace and Cyril continued their father's monumental task, expanding the number of views offered to the public and recording more and more places in Britain, as the coasts and countryside were opened up to mass travel. The archive Frith created

continued in business for another seventy years. By 1970 it contained over a third of a million pictures of 7,000 cities, towns and villages. The massive photographic record Frith has left to us stands as a living monument to a special and very remarkable man.

This book shows Haverfordwest as it was photographed by this world-famous archive at various periods in its development over the past 150 years. Every photograph was taken for a specific commercial purpose, which explains why the selection may not show every aspect of the town landscape. However, the photographs, compiled from one of the world's most celebrated archives, provide an important and absorbing record of your town.

"...the best buylt, the most civill and the quickest occupied Towne in south Wales"

LELAND, 1577

A HISTORY

ACCORDING to George Owen in 1603, the original settlement of Haverford, or Hwllfordd in Welsh, was one of three 'commots' in the cantref of Rhos; but Haverfordwest, or 'Haverford', had its origins in the Anglo-Norman period. The term 'cantref' simply signifies 100 villages and 'commot' or 'commote' indicates a neighbourhood.

As is often the case, the principal catalyst for the town's evolution into a busy commercial centre was the establishment of its castle. Artisans and traders built in the area immediately surrounding the castle, a decision driven by both commercial good sense and the need for security. We can still see the street patterns of this time reflected in today's Haverfordwest. As well as a town it was also a "county of itself" (George Owen, 1603), having had its unusual 'dual status' as both town and county granted by Royal charter in 1479.

Haverford was a sensible choice for this original military settlement. The rocky outcrop on which the castle stands overlooks the tidal reaches of the Western Cleddau river, navigable to commercial and military traffic and also providing an obstacle to a land invasion from this direction. The first documentary evidence tells us that a castle was built here by a Fleming, Tancred, in 1110. Many of his countrymen and women followed so a large Fleming settlement was

established in the area and the indigenous folk were simply driven away.

George Owen's 1603 account of this population movement goes as follows: "...about 1104 or 1105 a great part of the Low Countries, in Flanders, was suddenly overflown by the sea and never afterwards recovered, whereby the inhabitants of that place were sent by the Earl of Flanders to his cousin King Henry to seek habitations, for that diverse parts of England lay waste and wanted people ... [King Henry] thought better to send those Flemings thither [to Wales] to get their livings

This picture looking across the river into the town shows the Salutation Hotel in the centre and the castle dominating the horizon to the right.

by continual fighting with the Welshmen than spend his own men in that service. Wherefore the said Flemings were sent thither to Gerald, steward of Pembroke … [and] … were for the safeguard of themselves forced to begin to build the towns of Tenby, Pembroke and Haverfordwest."

The linguistic and cultural differences between these Flemish immigrants and their neighbours were obvious but integration did gradually take place, although some Pembrokeshire families were still speaking Flemish in the 16th century. Flemish gradually gave way to English. Welsh does not appear to have been the lingua franca in the area at any time.

The conditions for a thriving commercial centre were thus established - a secure military base and excellent river communications. The community thrived, and was only subject to sporadic attacks from the native Welsh. Tancred's daughters married well but he was succeeded by his son Richard fitzTancred whose son, Robert, is first mentioned in 1204.

Robert was granted the right to hold a Sunday market in the town in 1207, a lucrative concession and an

A HISTORY

indication of the increasing prosperity of the town. The Augustinian Priory was founded shortly before 1210 and gifted the incomes of the three churches of St Martin's, St Thomas's and St Mary's.

Robert fitzTancred fell out of favour with King John and in 1210 was deprived of all his holdings and was dead by 1211. In 1213 Haverford was granted to William Marshal ("a wise and a valiant nobleman" according to George Owen in 1603) who also held extensive lands in Ireland. Haverford thus became an important link between this lord's various properties and grew at a phenomenal rate through the 13th century. William Marshal I died by 1219 and he was succeeded by his sons William, who himself died in 1231, Richard (d 1234), Gilbert (d 1241), Walter (d 1244) and Anselm (d 1244).

Haverford largely escaped the attentions of marauding Welsh warlords while other towns, such as Carmarthen, were hard-pressed. The exception came in 1220 when Llywelyn the Great's army descended on the town, probably provoked by his animosity towards William Marshal II. The castle's strong defences prevented complete destruction, but Llywelyn burned the surrounding town. The town was quick to recover, but not the Marshal clan - all William Marshal's five sons died without male heirs and the estate reverted to William Marshal I's five daughters. The estate fell to Eva de Braose, but she was already dead and this meant that in 1246 the estate was split three ways among her children. One third of the estate, that now belonging to Eva and William de Cantiloupe, was assigned to Eleanor and Humphrey de Bohun who passed their two thirds share to their son Humphrey de Bohun II. The remaining third was held by Maud and Roger Mortimer, who subsequently passed their share to their daughter Matilda. This was to be no happy arrangement. From 1263 Roger Mortimer and Humphrey de Bohun took opposite sides in the Baron's

GENERAL VIEW 1890 27938

A group of turn-of-the-century children overlooking the town of Haverfordwest. The castle can be clearly seen on the right of the picture and the tower of St Mary's with one of its clock faces to the centre of the picture on the horizon.

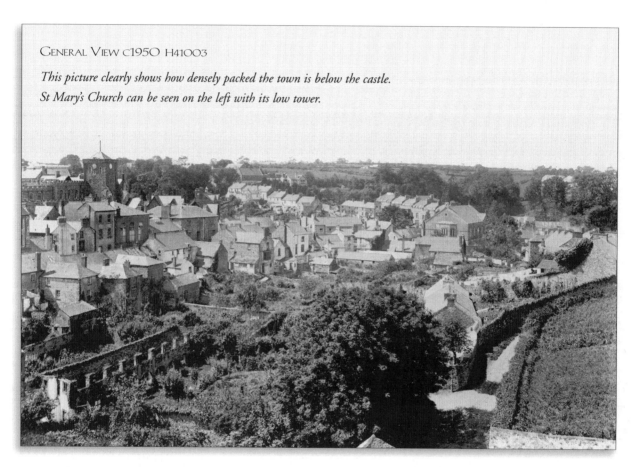

GENERAL VIEW C1950 H41003

This picture clearly shows how densely packed the town is below the castle.
St Mary's Church can be seen on the left with its low tower.

War with Mortimer siding with the Crown. The town was eventually besieged and captured from de Bohun by the King's brother, William de Valence. Disputes over the lordship of the town meant the King himself had to come to Haverford in 1284 to settle the issue.

In 1289 the town passed briefly into the ownership of Eleanor of Castile, the wife of Edward I. She died in 1290 but only after spending large amounts of money on the castle. The castle was largely in Royal hands from this point onwards. Edward I granted it to his son (later Edward II) who passed it on to Aymer de Valence, the Earl of Pembroke, in 1308. The castle reverted to the Crown after his death in 1324. Edward III gifted it to his mother, Isabella of France in 1331 and between then and her death in 1358 she retained ownership. Her son,

Edward the Black Prince, was in control of the castle from 1343.

The town was granted its charter of incorporation in 1479 and so acquired its mayor, sheriff and two bailiffs. By the middle of the 16th century the town was referred to as "the best buylt the most civill and quickest occupied Towne in south Wales…". Later in the town's history we encounter perhaps its greatest benefactor —Sir John Perrot.

"Know ye that I, the said Sir John Perrot, for the love which I bear towards my beloved and faithful neighbours, the burgesses of the town and county of Haverfordwest, and for the mayor, sheriff, bailiffs and burgesses of the said town, have granted for them and their successors … messuages, lands, tenements, burgages and hereditaments

… situate and lying as well in the town and county of Haverfordwest as in the said county of Pembroke…"

An interesting character, having a reputation as a brawler in his youth, Perrot nevertheless endowed the town with sufficient income (perhaps £30 per annum) to enable it to improve its infrastructure. It is also interesting to note that he was on extremely bad terms with one or two of these burgesses whom he professed to love! Conjecture as to Perrot's true motives in endowing the town in this way should be the subject of another book. In 1581 William Walter also established a fund for the improvement of the town but this sum seems to have been embezzled. Numerous other benefactors have funded the repair of churches, the establishment of schools and the relief of the town's poor.

In his 1603 book 'The Description of Pembrokeshire', George Owen commented that "The air of this county is said of strangers that resort thither from the inland parts of England to be very cold and piercing, but found to be very healthy to the county's inhabitants, seldom subject to infirmities, whereby the people live long and continue in very perfect of health and memory."

So, breathe deeply of this 'cold and piercing' Pembrokeshire air and let us explore the town of Haverfordwest. Before crossing the New Bridge and entering the medieval town, these photographs taken in the outlying village of Prendergast are worthy of note.

THE TOWN AND CASTLE 1906 53739

A splendid view of the town and castle. The Salutation Hotel pictured centre left is now the County Hotel. Some of the trees, newly-planted in this picture, still survive today.

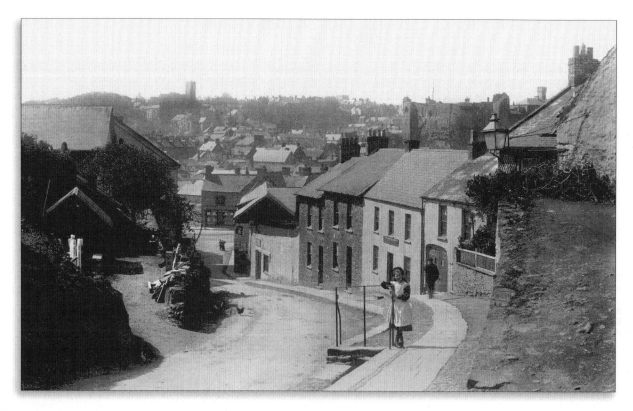

Above: THE TOWN FROM PRENDERGAST 1898 41078

Looking across the town into Haverfordwest, the tower of the Church of St Thomas à Becket can be clearly seen on the skyline towards the centre of the picture, and the main body of the Castle with its flagpole to the right.

Right: PRENDERGAST CHURCH 1898 41090

St David's, Prendergast, occupies a commanding position, overlooking the Cleddau River and the town of Haverfordwest.

SALUTATION SQUARE TO VICTORIA PLACE

THE main trunk roads to and from Fishguard, Milford Haven and Carmarthen all meet in Salutation Square and it is here we find the two War Memorials to the 1914-18 and 1939-45 wars. The 1914-18 memorial, commemorating the estimated 3,000 Pembrokeshire men who were killed during the First World War, was originally to be found in the middle of Salutation Square. It was dedicated on 3 September 1921. The 1939-45 plaques were relocated from nearby St Mary's church in 1954 to a position near to the 1914-18 memorial in order to facilitate the annual Cenotaph services.

SALUTATION SQUARE 1906 53747

A charming turn-of-the-century tableau of Salutation Square, the main access into the town. Note the hotel carriage by the entrance and the various horse-drawn conveyances. The fountain in the middle of the square has now been removed and this is now a busy road junction. The chapel with the colonnaded frontage is now 'RJ's Nitespot'.

SALUTATION SQUARE TO VICTORIA PLACE

Above: SALUTATION SQUARE C1950 H41032

The war memorial pictured here, crowned with a symbolic Welsh dragon, was moved from this position in 1973. The building to the left has been removed and this is where the memorial can be found. The inscription reads: '1914-1918. In remembrance of the men of the county of Pembroke, who at the call of King and country left all that was dear to them, endured hardness, faced dangers and finally passed out of the sight of men by the path of duty and self-sacrifice, giving up their own lives that others might live in freedom. Let those who come after see to it that their names be not forgotten.' Note that the hotel to the right, once the Salutation Hotel, is now the County Hotel.

Opposite Top: SALUTATION SQUARE C1960 H41080

Another view of Salutation Square before its redevelopment and transformation into a busy road junction. The board on the 'Keep Left' sign refers to a Royal Army Ordnance Corps exercise.

Opposite Below: THE TOWN FROM THE NEW BRIDGE 1890 27945

This view looking from the New to the Old Bridge is now much altered. A footbridge now spans the river between the two and there has been extensive development on both banks of the river. The channel leading up to where the boat sits at its mooring is no longer in evidence. Note the piles of rubble deposited onto the bank, perhaps early in-fill as this part of the river is built up after this date and by 1960 has evolved into a car park.

SALUTATION SQUARE TO VICTORIA PLACE

THE NEW BRIDGE 1890 27948

The wall on the left on which the child is sitting has since been extensively redeveloped as the river frontage for a shopping development. It is now a series of steps leading down to the water. Out of sight and beyond the bridge to the left is the new County Hall.

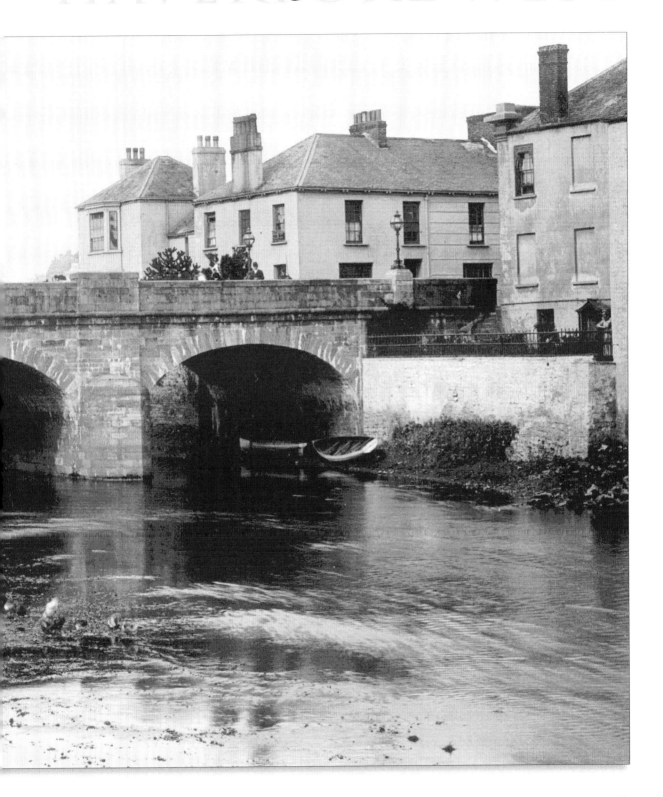

THE RIVER CLEDDAU
c1960 H41067

*Looking down towards the
Old Bridge this is barely
recognisable today. Note that
since 1890 (see picture 27945)
the area to the right where the
Pickfords lorry is has now been
completely in-filled and the
river has its present-day course.*

THE NEW BRIDGE AND HIGH STREET c1955 H41039

*Looking across the bridge up the High Street, the building to the left is now the Haverfordwest Property Centre. The
Prudential, shown on the right is now the West Wales Property Company.*

Above: THE NEW BRIDGE c1955
H41038

Looking back across the bridge towards Salutation Square. The Cavendish County Theatre to the right has since been demolished and this area is now the site of the new County Offices.

Left: THE COUNTY THEATRE AND PICTON PLACE c1950 H41030

The Cavendish can be seen here on the right. Note the absence of road markings and the apparently low volume of traffic that enables motorists to park on the bridge itself. Picton Place is named after the Picton family, referred to later.

SALUTATION SQUARE TO VICTORIA PLACE

After passing through Picton Place with the new County Offices on our left, the road into the town crosses the Western Cleddau via the New Bridge and passes into Victoria Place. This 'new' bridge was part of the 19th century effort to modernised the town and make it more accessible. The river is referred to as the 'White Cleddau' ('Cleddau Wen') by George Owen in 'The Description of Pembrokeshire'.

By 1835, the date of the Municipal Reform Act, Haverfordwest was improving the approaches to the town, installing lighting, supplying water to the town and also undertaking resurfacing work along the streets and pavements. The bridge itself was apparently financed to the tune of £2,000 by one William Owen. He was to eventually recover some of his money from the bridge's tollgates.

VICTORIA PLACE C1950 H41031

The Lloyds Bank to the left of the road is still in existence and bears a commemorative plaque to Gwen John and her brother Augustus John, both artists. Gwen was born in Haverfordwest on 22 June 1876 and died 1 September 1939. Augustus was born in Tenby where the family, normally resident in the town, were escaping an outbreak of an infectious disease. He lived in Haverfordwest from 1878 to 1874 and died in October 1961.

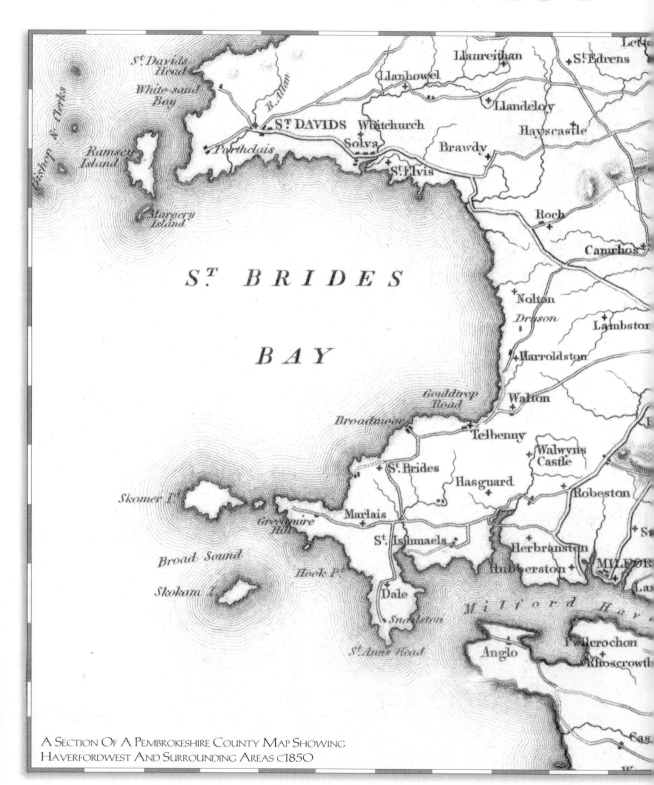

A SECTION OF A PEMBROKESHIRE COUNTY MAP SHOWING
HAVERFORDWEST AND SURROUNDING AREAS c1850

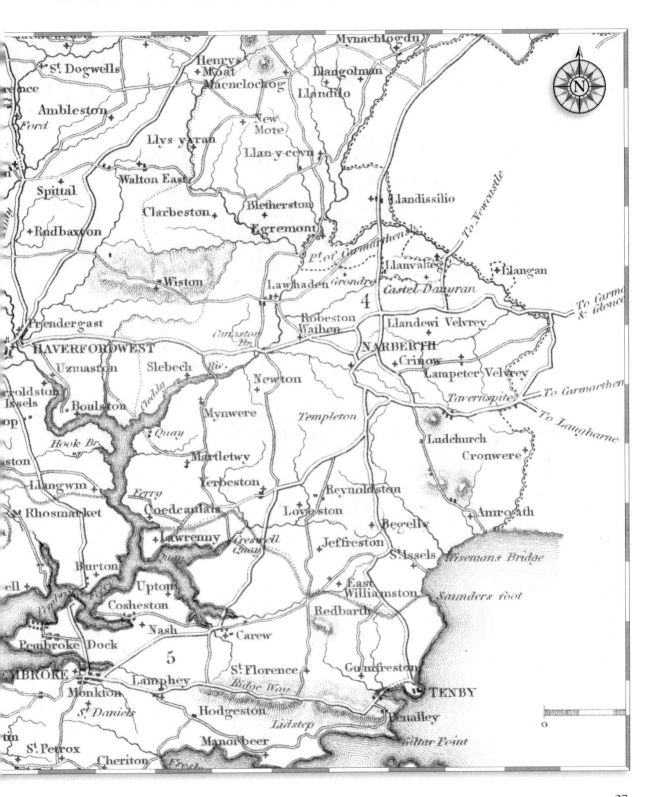

CASTLE SQUARE, QUAY STREET, THE RIVER AND PRIORY

CASTLE SQUARE c1950 H41033

The Lloyds Bank on the left is still in place today but the Boots beyond it has been relocated to the new shopping development on the riverside. The Castle Hotel on the right is much the same today with the exception of the crenellations to the right. The traffic lights are no longer here, the road being one-way.

CASTLE SQUARE, QUAY STREET, THE RIVER AND PRIORY

THE LEFT turn from Castle Square is Quay Street. It may have originally been named 'Schippistrete', first mentioned in 1370, or 'Key Street' mentioned in 1564. The new Post Office was relocated here from the High Street in 1936. As well as the many buildings connected with the river trade, there were also mills and a fish weir along the river here. The port was undoubtedly a significant one, not merely confined to coastal trade but with links to Europe and Ireland as well. It seems that ships of fairly large tonnage (up to 40 tons) would have used the port, from two-masted ships to flat-bottomed barges used for river traffic. Ships from Gascogny and even Portugal would have been found docked at the quay unloading their cargoes of salt, wine and other goods.

Even as late as 1831 the river saw a prodigious amount of commercial traffic. Wheat, barley and oats were regularly exported to cities such as Liverpool and London, and imports of salt, wine, iron and sugar were frequently landed here from France, Portugal and Spain. Even though the international dimension of the town's trade diminished after that time there still remained healthy trading relationships with many Irish ports, Bristol, London and Liverpool. An echo of this trading past can be seen in the 'Bristol Trader' public house in Quay Street.

The Moravian church met in a building in Quay Street before relocating to their premises on St Thomas's Green and there were also Quaker meetings held in a warehouse here before the building of a Meeting House on the corner of Quay Street and High Street. The Quakers

CASTLE SQUARE, QUAY STREET, THE RIVER AND PRIORY

Above: THE RIVER 1890 27947

The buildings to the left are the river side of Quay Street and served as port facilities for the town. Quay Street was also once known as 'Schippistrete', a very descriptive title. The castle can be seen in the centre of the picture. The Moravians once held meetings in a building in the street before relocating uphill to St Thomas's Green.

Right: THE TOWN FROM THE RAILWAY 1890 27936A

This photograph was taken looking across the railway and the western Cleddau river onto Quay Street and the town and castle beyond. It was the arrival of the railway that sounded the death knell for the old port of Haverfordwest. The South Wales Railway reached the town in 1854.

Castle Square, Quay Street, the River and Priory

Left: Quay Street 1906 53750

This scene is barely recognisable today. Note the clothing drying on the railing and the unmade road. This would have been dusty in summer and a quagmire in winter, especially with the heavy horse-drawn traffic that would have moved up and down this street to load and unload the vessels moored along the quay.

Below: The Priory Ruins 1890 27951

The Augustinian Priory of St Mary and St Thomas the Martyr was founded c1200 by Robert fitz Richard (d 1213). The three medieval churches of St Mary's, St Thomas à Becket and St Martin's were all gifted to the Priory by Robert and must have been a significant source of income. The Priory was closed in 1536 at the time of the Dissolution of the Monasteries. Note the lady on the right of the picture carrying the earthenware jug, and the railway bridge across the western Cleddau.

CASTLE SQUARE, QUAY STREET, THE RIVER AND PRIORY

were particularly troublesome for the town authorities in the aftermath of the Civil Wars when the radical dissenting groups were in full voice. In 1659 one William Bateman challenged the doctrines of the preacher at St Mary's and he was later prosecuted for holding unauthorised meetings in his house. In 1662, 13 of their number were imprisoned for not removing their hats in deference to the authorities in the Guildhall. Numbers attending the Quaker meetings declined and the building was eventually demolished in 1835 and formed part of the site of the Shire Hall.

Further along the bank of the Western Cleddau,

we come to the ruins of the Augustinian Priory of St Mary and St Thomas the Martyr. This evidently once-prosperous establishment is yet another indication of the rapid growth of the town in the early medieval period. It was itself a stimulus for growth. Endowed with the incomes of the town's three parish churches, the castle chapel, the tithes of fitz Tancred's wool, cheese, mills and lands around the town, the Priory was built on foundations which were more solid financially than physically. Being sited on the banks of a navigable river and near to the town's quay facilities were definite advantages, but the ground sloped down to an area of marshland and the Western Cleddau,

THE TOWN FROM PRIORY HILL 1890 27944

A panoramic view of the town with the Priory ruins in the foreground and the tower of the church of St Thomas à Becket on the hill to the left. The Castle can be seen in the centre.

CASTLE SQUARE, QUAY STREET, THE RIVER AND PRIORY

being tidal, was prone to flooding here. The problem was overcome by excavating into the slope above the flood-line and using the spoil to in-fill below it. The finished Priory was conventional both in terms of size and layout and even its location by the side of a busy commercial port is characteristic of other Augustinian houses in Wales and England. Also in keeping with other establishments this Priory was virtually autonomous, although it was subject to the diocesan authority.

By the time it was dissolved in 1536, the Priory held even more extensive lands and incomes. Lead was stripped from the windows, stonework was removed and any reusable blocks of stone were recovered for further use. As with so many similar sites, pillaging of the remaining stonework for a variety of building projects over the subsequent years would have robbed the site still further. All that eventually remained of the Priory was a series of ivy-clad masonry towers (as can be seen in 27951) until the site was acquired by the Guild of Freemen of Haverfordwest who gave it to the Secretary of State for Wales so that an extensive programme of renovation could begin.

THE VIEW FROM THE EAST 1948 H41008

An excellent view of the post-WWII town looking across the railway lines into the town. Note the many railway wagons in the yards in the foreground of the picture. The spire of St Martin's church can be seen to the right of the castle.

ST THOMAS'S CHURCH

IN WINCH LANE we pass the site of the old Workhouse, Priory Mount, which was built here between 1837 and 1839. It was converted into flats in 1982. The site of the County War Memorial Hospital is on the right, and then we go on towards St Thomas's.

Haverfordwest's third church, dedicated to St Thomas à Becket, was for many years on the fringes of the town. The murdered Thomas was canonized in 1173, which at least tells us that the first structure was built sometime after that. It was demolished and rebuilt during the 17th century apart from one wall and the tower. By 1851 the building was in need of extensive repair and when these repairs were completed, at a cost of £1,200, the building was reopened in 1855 by the Bishop of St David's. Work on the churchyard was also undertaken and completed in 1857. It is interesting to note that iron railings and gates were supplied by Stephen Green; Stephen and Fred Green's High Street shop front can be seen c1950 in H41017, page 38, and c1955 in H41037, page 40, and H41040, page 39.

Close to the church, on St Thomas's Green, we find the site of the former Moravian church. The Moravians were a group of Christian refugees from persecution in their native Bohemia who found a safe haven in

St Thomas's Church 1898 41085

Properly named the parish church of St Thomas à Becket, this church was obviously founded after the murdered prelate was canonized. It is first mentioned in records in 1210.

St Thomas's Church

Saxony. Possessing missionary zeal, they were soon dispatching missionaries to many European countries, including England and Wales. The Moravian church in Haverfordwest, the earliest Moravian gathering in south Wales, was opened in 1763 and, after initially meeting in premises on Quay Street, purchased a property on St Thomas's Green. A purpose-built chapel was built in 1773 which finally closed in 1957 and a block of sheltered housing - Moravian Court - now stands on the site.

St Thomas's Green was also the site of the town's gaol which, after the building of the new gaol in the castle's outer ward, was converted into a lunatic asylum, the first county asylum in Wales but by 1835 it was thought to be inadequate to the task.

From here the Parade leads back towards the town centre. The views from here are now largely obstructed by trees, but must once have been impressive; but walking down the steps into Hill Lane (listed as 'Batemanys Lane' in 1471) still provides yet another excellent view of the town.

St Thomas's Church
INTERIOR 1898 41091

The church has been much re-built and re-designed over the years. It was demolished and rebuilt in the 17th century and effectively rebuilt in 1854-5 and again in 1880-1. This latest set of modifications included the installation of the seven-bay arcade between nave and aisle pictured here, a new stained glass window above the altar and new floor tiles.

The Town from the
Parade 1890 27946

This panoramic view of the town from the Parade is now largely obscured by trees and the path is now tarmacadam.

HILL LANE, HIGH STREET AND MARKET STREET

TURNING LEFT into the High Street, the lower part of which was sufficiently wide in medieval times to allow a row of eight shops and/or houses to be built in the middle of the street known as 'Short Row'. They were removed to make way for the approach road to the new bridge (Victoria Place) after 1834. The town's main streets have been a bustling commercial centre for centuries. There are references to the halls of various craft guilds, such as the Shoemakers' and the Feltmakers', from 1580 onwards.

HILL LANE AND THE CASTLE 1906 53740

Another interesting scene of the town taken from the steps in Hill Lane looking towards the castle. Note the new prison (built 1820) to the left of the main castle buildings with its chimneys and observation tower, all of which have been removed. The roof today is modern and sports a series of roof-lights. This view today is much the same as pictured here. The gateway in the stone wall (centre left) is now a garage door. The Millar Tobacconist at the foot of the hill beyond the horse and cart is now Castle Photography.

HILL LANE, HIGH STREET AND MARKET STREET

Below: HIGH STREET c1950 H41017

The Castle Hotel is to the right of this picture. Note the shop frontage for Stephen and Fred Green on the left (now a chartered accountants). The authors have learned from Mr W David Thomas that the Ford car 'EDE 3' belonged to his late father Mr William Gwyther Thomas, the Divisional Highways Surveyor. The reason for it being apparently abandoned in the middle of the road was that the traffic lights had failed and Mr Thomas was investigating the reason at the control box. The sign on the lamp post indicates that the Post Office can be found in Quay Street, to where it was moved from the corner of High Street and Dark Street in 1936. The RAC sign on the Castle Hotel has now been removed - the hotel is currently with the AA! The building to the left of the picture is the home of the Crown and Magistrates' Courts.

Opposite: HIGH STREET c1955 H41040

Looking down the High Street towards the river and Salutation Square. Note the tobacconist on the left advertising Players No 3 and the canisters outside Stephen & Fred Green on the right (now a menswear shop and a branch of OXFAM).

HILL LANE, HIGH STREET AND MARKET STREET

The privilege of trading in the busy town would have been strictly protected - only burgesses of the town and guild members would have been allowed to trade and others would have been prosecuted. This was also the position of the old Post Office until its removal in 1936 to Quay Street. This Post Office was also a terminal for the Atlantic cable, so the town was often among the first in Britain to receive news of international importance.

Market Street, to the left, was first mentioned in 1491 as 'Pillerestret', or 'Pillorie Streete'. The town's markets would have been significant sources of income for the townsfolk and would have been held in the environs of St Mary's church and in this street. A small market was held on Tuesdays and a much larger event was held on Saturdays. Goods of every description would be sold at these events including meat, fish, tools and clothing. George Owen said of Pembrokeshire in

1603 that "…this little county … is not without plenty of God's blessing as well for sufficient means for the people to live in good and plentiful sort as also to vend and send into other countries, thereby bringing in money to procure such necessaries from other countries as the same wants." Haverfordwest was particularly well-placed to benefit from 'God's blessing' to the county and was one of three market towns in the county, the others being Pembroke and Tenby. Owen describes Haverfordwest market as "one of the greatest and plentifullest markets (all things compared) that is within the Marches of Wales, especially for the plenty and goodness of victual, as namely for beef, mutton, pork, bacon, veal, goose, capon, kid, lamb, coney, turkey and all sorts of wildfowl in their season … And for fish it passes all others in Wales, without any comparison, both for plenty and variety."

Hill Lane, High Street and Market Street

HIGH STREET C1955 H41037

The clock, just past Stephen & Fred Green belongs to Bisley H Munt & Son, jewellers, established 1796 (according to the inscription on the clock-face), and it can still be found. The Midland Bank beyond it is now HSBC and the cycle shop opposite is now the offices for the Pembrokeshire Coast National Park.

Hill Lane, High Street and Market Street

MARKET STREET 1898 41080

Taken from the junction of Market Street and Upper Market Street looking down towards the High Street.

UPPER HIGH STREET C1950 H41019

Looking up towards St Mary's Church. Note the unmarked roads. A branch of Stead and Simpson, a shoe shop, is on the right directly opposite Cash & Co, also a shoe shop. Below and to the right of St Mary's Church we can see the gable end of the Old Post Office. Built in 1880, it fulfilled this role until 1936 when the mail and counter services were moved to Quay Street. To its front, and just to the left of the bay window is the William Nichol Memorial, which reads: "The noble army of Martyrs, praise thee. On this spot William Nichol, of this town was burnt at the stake for the truth, April 9th 1558." William Nichol was one of the Marian Martyrs who died as a result of the purges instigated by 'Bloody' Mary, the Catholic Queen of England. The present memorial, a Balmoral red granite column erected in 1912, supersedes a large stone (known as the 'Martyr Stone') which has since been taken to Dale Castle.

HILL LANE, HIGH STREET AND MARKET STREET

With the overseas and coastal trades accessible via the Western Cleddau and the fertile agricultural hinterland in the opposite direction, Haverfordwest was a veritable magnet for those wishing to buy or sell a wide variety of goods. There were also a number of annual fairs, for example, the Bartholomew Fair which was first held in 1610. George Owen mentions a fair on 7 July, St Thomas's Day and describes it as "A great fair". There were many other fairs on the town's calendar, including a wool fair in June and a hiring fair in October.

A right turn into Hill Street (the lower part of which was known as 'Short Row' in 1427) takes us past the former Corn Market on the left. This is one of Haverfordwest's finest surviving Victorian buildings and was built in the mid-1850s at a cost of around £700. It was a risky enterprise - seen as daring to those in approval and reckless to those in opposition. It was a considerable success over the following half-century. Now a cinema, the building also acted as the headquarters of the Pembrokeshire Fire Brigade and was where the count for a number of elections was carried out.

Further up the street, also on the left, is a commemorative plaque to General Sir Thomas Picton, one of the town's most famous sons. Born in Hill Street (where The Dragon public house now is), he studied at the Grammar School and then joined the army at the age of 13. After a

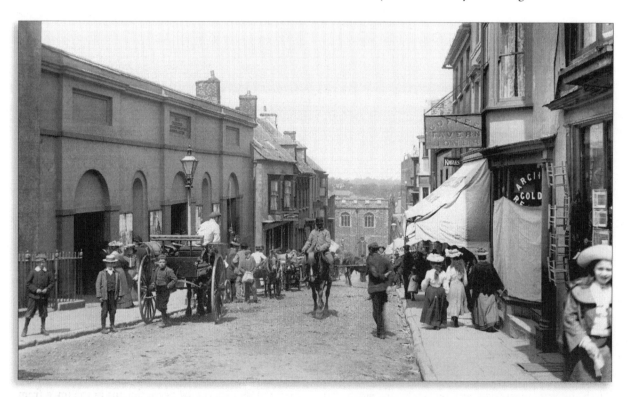

MARKET STREET 1906 53744

A busy scene looking down towards the High Street. Note the unmarked and unmade road, the baby high chairs on sale on the right, the coffee tavern beyond it and Olivers, the boot and shoe chain, further down the street on the right. Note also that in these days no-one, from the oldest to the youngest, would be seen out without a hat.

HILL LANE, HIGH STREET AND MARKET STREET

MARKET STREET 1907 53745

A splendid view of this busy street with plenty of interested onlookers to pose for the camera. Olivers, the early boot and shoe retailer, is on the left with its wares on show all around the doorway. Two doors on is a depot for the Society for the Promotion of Christian Knowledge. Note the man on the right erecting a blind and the horse with its cart patiently waiting for Mr. Frith to finish his work.

brief period of military inactivity he was called back to duty to serve in the Napoleonic Wars. Commanding the 'Fighting Division' he achieved a heroic reputation during the struggle to free Europe from Napoleon's dominance. When preparing to storm the walls at Badajoz during the Peninsular War he is quoted as saying: "If we cannot win the castle let us die upon its wall". This seems to have been interpreted as encouragement by his troops, as they succeeded. After the resumption of conflict when Napoleon returned from exile, Picton was once again in the heat of battle. Wounded at Quatre Bras on 16 June 1815, he was nonetheless leading his troops again two days later at the Battle of Waterloo where he was killed.

Shipman's Lane is to the right, and right again is Dew Street, first mentioned in the late 13th century as Dewystret, after St David, the patron saint of Wales.

This street was so wide (by medieval standards) that an 'island' of small houses or even shops was built in the middle of the road. This was known as 'Middle Row' in a lease of 1664 and is also possibly the 'Rat Island' which was demolished in 1845. On the right roughly halfway down Dew Street is the site of the former 'Pig Bank' where a pig market was held until just before the Second World War.

On the left of Dew Street is the site of the former Grammar School. This venerable establishment served the community for almost 500 years. We know that there was an educational establishment in the town from as early as 1488 and past venues have been St Thomas's Church and Church Lane (in 1761, with 50 boys). The school pictured in 53748, page 45, was built in 1856 at a cost of £1,350. It was on this site until 1965.

43

HILL LANE, HIGH STREET AND MARKET STREET

MARKET STREET c1950
H41027

MARKET STREET c1950
H41027

Looking down Market Street towards St Mary's with the spire of St Martin's just visible beyond. The shop names visible on the right, moving right to left are Charles Saies, draper; Herbert, ironmonger; Picture Post; the County Stores and Oliver's. Across the street is the Élite Salon and Sidney Heath.

HILL LANE, HIGH STREET AND MARKET STREET

Above: DEW STREET 1906 53748

The building in the centre of the picture was the former butter and fish market. Dating from 1791 this two-storey building served this purpose until 1900 when the ground floor became a municipal dairy and the upper storey the repository of the Council records. It was demolished in 1951 and was then the site of the 1939-45 War Memorial until this was moved to Salutation Square. The building on the left was the former grammar school and was demolished and is now the site of the library. The steeply-angled gable end with bellcote beyond the grammar school is that of the Roman Catholic Church of St. David and St Patrick, opened in 1872. The tower of St Mary's Church can been seen beyond the butter and fish market.

Opposite: HILL STREET 1906 53742

Formerly named 'Hill of St Thomas' or 'Hilstret', it runs from St Thomas's Green to Market Street. Note the 'parked' carts to the left and the busy traffic!

FROM ST MARY'S TO ST MARTIN'S

IN photograph 27950 (opposite) the Mariners Hotel is on the right and there is a good view of the former Borough Police Station, previously a charnel house, centre left at the top of the cobbled street.

The lower story was barrel-vaulted and the building was used as the police station from 1835. In 1836 the Station was manned by a sergeant and two or three men. In 1888, shortly before this photograph was taken, the police station was moved to the Castle and the building was later demolished to allow for road widening. Note the beer barrels on the right ready for collection, and also the posters advertising "Ceylon Tea ... Try It".

ST MARY'S CHURCH 1898 41087

An excellent view of the gable end of this church showing the 13th century lancet windows and above them the roof-line of the original nave. The church was re-built c1220 and was once graced with a tower (subsequently removed and not replaced, hence its rather stunted appearance).

Left: ST MARY'S CHURCH, THE CHANCEL
1899 43634

Founded in the late 1100s, St Mary's was re-roofed in oak at the beginning of the 16th century. Pictured here is the east window, three lights with quatrefoils in roundels above each one. The beautiful four-bay arcade in the main body of the church is of exceptional quality and sports a variety of images including an ape playing a harp and a pig playing a fiddle!

Below: ST MARY'S CHURCH
1890 27950

Dominating this area of the town is St Mary's Church. The siting of this church dedicated to St Mary is enigmatic, but was possibly built near to a re-sited market place in the late 12th century. The building was originally graced with an impressive leaded spire and was perhaps the finest of the three in the town. Its bells would have rung out over the town adding its peal to those of St Martin's, St Thomas's, the Friary and, we assume, those of the Priory as well.

Nearby is a surviving medieval structure known as 'The Crypt'. Theories as to its use are plentiful but one strong contender is that it was a 'charnel vault' to store bones from the overcrowded graveyard. It was almost lost in the interests of road improvements, but fortunately an alternative scheme was settled on. The churchyard was once the setting for the town's thriving markets until townsfolk complained about the large number of butchers' stalls in the churchyard and in 1773 the churchwardens and the mayor went so far as to prevent the traders from entering the churchyard. A legal battle ensued, but the stalls were eventually relocated. A large purpose-built market house was opened in 1825.

FROM ST MARY'S TO ST MARTIN'S

FROM ST MARY'S TO ST MARTIN'S

St Mary's has undergone several periods of renovation and in 1843 some schoolboys accidentally knocked some plaster off the arcade to reveal capitals of exceptional quality. A subscription fund was established to carry out the ensuing restoration and the building was reopened in 1844. After the spire was removed in 1802 numerous schemes were drawn up to restore the building's former grandeur and in 1860 it was hoped to add a further 20 feet in order to give it a 'minster-like appearance'. The plan did not come to fruition and the tower remained as we see it today.

Near to this point was the former Guild Hall, or 'gildhus' and there are also many references to the market activities in this area until 1827 when the new building was constructed in Market Street.

On the corner of Dark Street is the site of the former Assembly Rooms, now converted to flats, at which many evening entertainments were held. Built in the 18th century on the site of the former White Hart Inn, these rooms were the scene of much jollity, particularly during Hunt Week when balls would be held nightly. In 1925 the rooms were leased by the trustees of the Picton Estate for use as a church hall for nearby St Mary's. By 1970 the building was deemed unsafe and was left unoccupied for some time. It was again sold in 1997 and has since been converted into flats.

ST MARY'S CHURCH C1955 H41054

The tower was capped by a timber spire until 1802, when it was removed at the behest of Lady Kensington who feared that it would fall on her nearby house. The issue of how, when and in what way the tower should be reinstated to its former glory is not resolved to this day. The clock faces on the tower were installed in 1885 at the expense of the Perrot Charity.

Opposite this is the former Tasker's School. Tasker's High School for Girls was a counterpart to the all-boys Grammar School in Dew Street. Named after Mrs Mary Tasker for her 1684 bequest for the foundation of a charity school for girls and boys, it occupied a variety of sites and became girl-only in 1882. In 1892 it was providing education for 92 girls from Haverfordwest and its surrounds.

The turning left past the Tasker's School is Barn Street. This part of the town, together with Dew Street and parts of Castleton, was largely abandoned as a result of the depletion in the population resulting from the Black Death. After the 1349 outbreak the town's population declined steeply, together with the revenues from trade. On the right further down this road is the impressive Romanesque frontage of the Bethesda Baptist Chapel with its large wheel window, arched windows to each side and extensive carved stonework. The chapel was not always as seen today, having undergone a series of demolitions, re-buildings and renovations. Work started in 1878 and the present Chapel, seating 900, was completed in 1880 at a cost of £2,199.

MARINER'S SQUARE 1906 53751

In the shadow of St Mary's Church, Hotel Mariners on the right was established in 1625. The building to the centre is now without its bay window. Note the sign on the left advertising Cadbury's chocolate and the cobbled street leading up to the church.

FROM ST MARY'S TO ST MARTIN'S

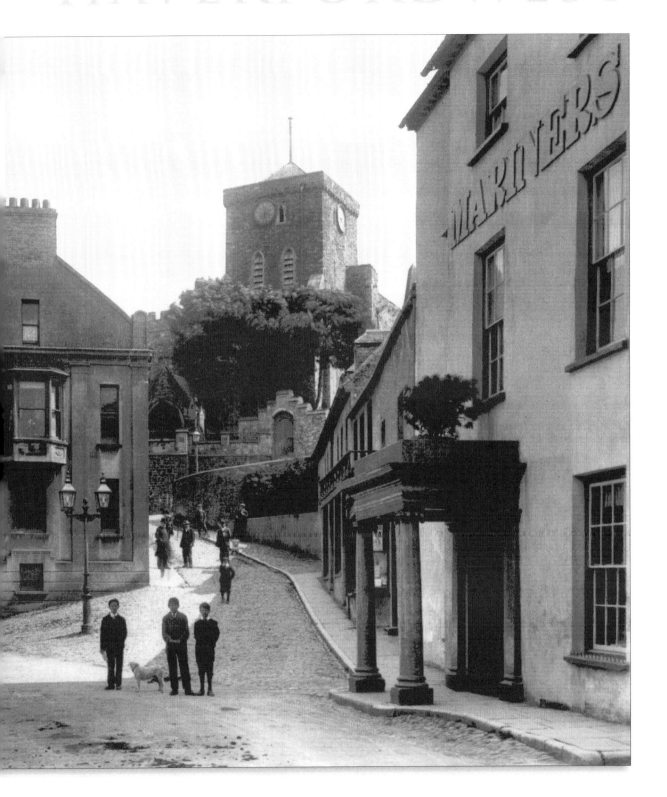

FROM ST MARY'S TO ST MARTIN'S

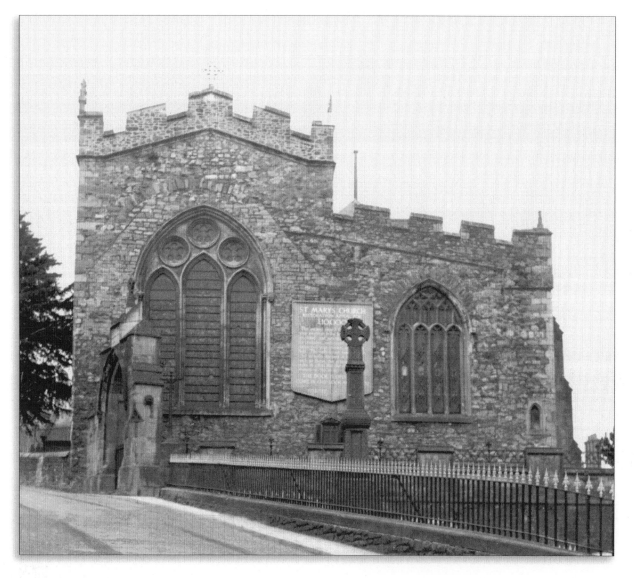

Above: ST MARY'S CHURCH C1960 H41060

After the famous invasion of French troops at Fishguard in 1797 the church was used as a prison for some of the captured French troops. A contemporary account in 'The Star', says the prisoners "wholly destroyed the inside of the church". Note the board between the windows appealing for £10,000 for the restoration of the building.

Opposite: ST MARY'S CHURCH C1950 H41034

By the time this photograph was taken building to the left of the picture had been painted and deprived of its bay window. The street is now tarmacadam.

FROM ST MARY'S TO ST MARTIN'S

THE HOTEL MARINERS c1950 H41035

The entrance portico of this hotel is rather dilapidated in this picture, which gives a somewhat false impression of the extensive additions to the hotel behind what is seen in this photograph.

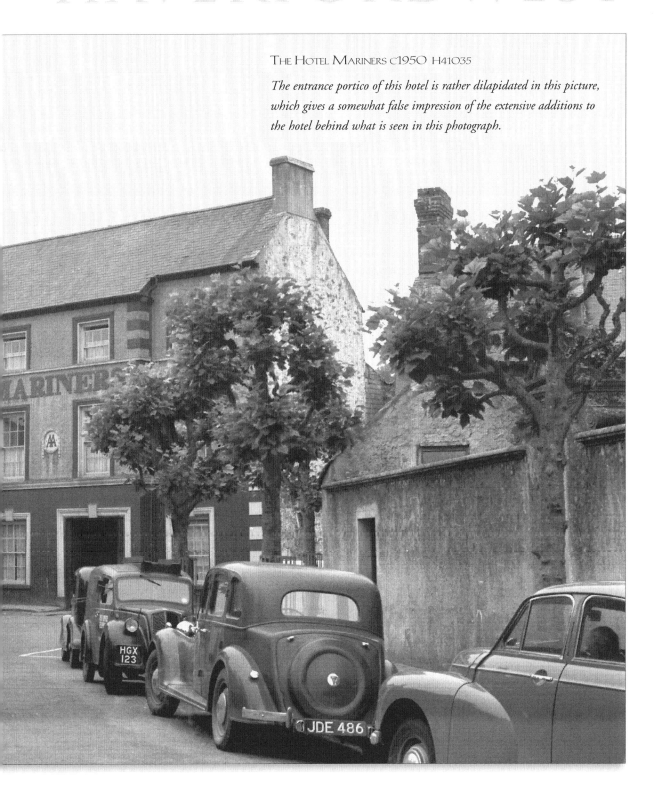

From St Mary's to St Martin's

FROM ST MARY'S TO ST MARTIN'S

Also in 27949, page 58, immediately beyond the Bethesda Baptist Chapel can be seen another medieval parish church - St Martin of Tours - which, with its proximity to the castle, is perhaps the oldest of the town's three medieval churches. It is situated in the medieval township of Castleton and overlooks Queen's Square, possibly itself the site of the earliest market (12th century) in Haverfordwest.

The fabric of the building began to decay from the 17th century onwards and was also the victim of much misguided 'renovation'. The church was in a serious state of disrepair by 1862 and extensive repairs were conducted until 1865 in response to an appeal for funds.

Looking down Barn Street towards the spire of St Martin's Church, the Bethesda Baptist Chapel can be seen on the right. The elaborate wrought-iron façade on the building on the left is still in existence and sports a beautiful wisteria. Note the Victorian street lamps.

ST MARTIN'S CHURCH AND BETHESDA CHAPEL 1890 27949

The Bethesda Baptist Chapel is seen in all its glory on the right. This site at the foot of Barn Street was purchased in 1789 for £200 and by September of that year a chapel costing £308 6s was complete. It was rebuilt in 1816 but damaged in a gas explosion in 1842. Work on the present chapel was completed in 1880 at a cost of £2,199. Note the 'I. Roberts, Merchant' sign on the left (now a house) and the advertising hoarding for Singer sewing machines on the building beyond the junction (now replaced).

FROM ST MARY'S TO ST MARTIN'S

Above: ST MARTIN'S CHURCH 1898 41088

This church, dedicated to St Martin of Tours, is the oldest of the town's three medieval churches and was built in the 12th century settlement of Castleton. Rebuilt in the early 14th century, the spire pictured here dates from 1870 and is about 15 feet higher than its predecessor.

Left: ST MARTIN'S CHURCH, INTERIOR 1898 41089

This photograph of the lovely interior of the church gives a good indication of how the former decay in the fabric of the church described in 1779 by Thomas Beaufort as "a large, old, ugly wretched church" has been reversed.

ORDNANCE SURVEY MAP

An Ordnance Survey Map showing Haverfordwest
and Surrounding Areas c1887

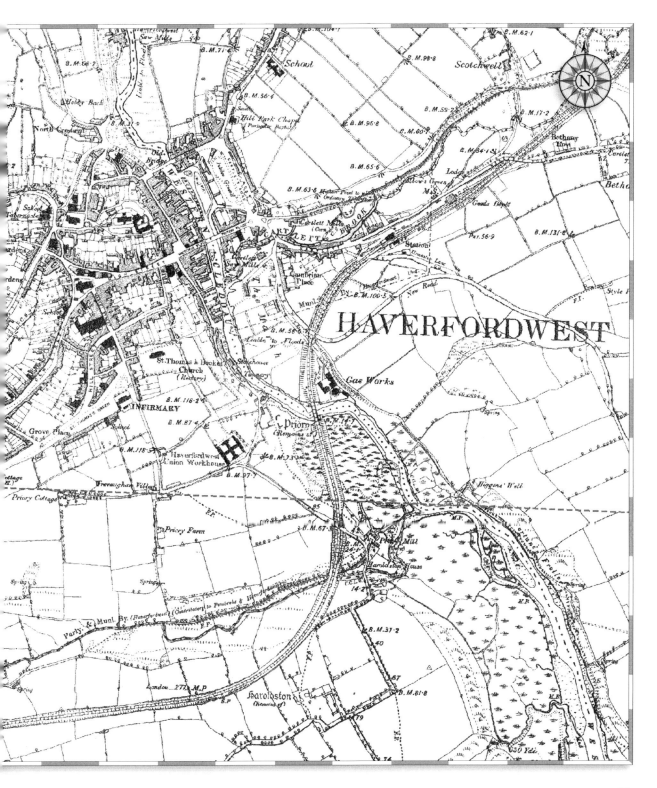

THE OLD BRIDGE

Right: BRIDGEND SQUARE 1906 53746

This area is now the site of a bus station. Corn and Butler is presently the Tourist Information Centre. The yard to the left no longer exists and this view of the castle is largely obscured by the new public toilets!

Below: THE OLD BRIDGE 1906 53752

Below Right: THE OLD BRIDGE AND CASTLE c1950 H41005

An excellent view of the Old Bridge with the castle in the background. The Fishguard Arms can be found at the end of the bridge but the horizontal sign is gone and has been replaced by a hanging board and the entrance to the pub is now via a slated portico. The foliage to the right is now buildings.

THE OLD BRIDGE

THE OLD BRIDGE c1945 H41001

The buildings seen to the right of the bridge here have been extensively redeveloped with the exception of the building with the bay window which remains as it is in this photograph. Modern lighting has been installed on the bridge.

THE OLD BRIDGE

FROM Bridgend Square the Old Bridge stretches across the Cleddau. A chapel was once located at the end of this bridge for the benefit of travellers.

Bridge Street, leading back towards the town centre, was referred to as 'Brygestret' in 1312 and was the location of the Friary of Dominican 'Blackfriars' founded by Robert de Hwllfordd. In 1256 the Blackfriars were granted the sum of £10 to relocate their buildings to a position between Bridge Street and the river where it underwent considerable expansion to the point where it may well have occupied this entire parcel of land. This position was latterly occupied by the Marychurch Foundry. Named after the founding family, the foundry was established by Solomon Marychurch in the second half of the 18th century. The firm expanded and during its career as a foundry it manufactured a wide range of ironmongery. From 1870 it was also producing ships' boilers and the company was a major employer in the town. It finally closed its doors in the mid-1930s.

The plaque to be found on the monument in the centre of Haverfordwest's old bridge reads:

'This bridge was erected at the sole expence [sic.] of Sir John Philipps of Picton Caftle, Bart. Anno 1726. Michale Prust Esqr. Mayor: In memory whereof This monument was Set Up by The Mayor and Council. Repaired by order of the Mayor and Corporation AD 1829 in the 10th Year of the Reign of His Majesty George the Fourth who Passed over this Bridge on His return from Ireland the 13th day of September 1821. This Bridge was Widened and Repaired in the year 1848 under the direction of the Magistrates, of the County and Town of Haverfordwest, at the expence of said County.'

THE OLD BRIDGE

THE OLD BRIDGE c1965 H41072

The lower water level is revealing more of the bridge piers. 'Thomas Butcher' to the right has been redeveloped and the steps are no longer to be seen.

THE CASTLE

HAVERFORDWEST was an obvious choice of location for the castle. The Western Cleddau is navigable to this point and also able to be bridged. In its life it has also housed a series of prison facilities for the county and town.

In 1405 there was a serious threat to the castle with the French invasion of the area in support of Owain Glyndwr's rebellion. They burned the town and attacked the castle but were beaten off with considerable losses. The defenders were perhaps aided by the hasty improvements that had been made to the castle's defences - the town was certainly not possessed by any kind of 'siege mentality' and its defences (with the evident exception of those of the castle itself) were certainly not regarded as formidable and offered no serious obstacle to Owain and his French allies.

THE CASTLE C1960 H41077

The Prison Governor's House, now the home of the excellent Town Museum, built in 1779 at the same time as the first prison, was built within the castle precinct. Note the police motor cycles on the left outside the former prison which became the headquarters of the Pembrokeshire Police from 1888 until 1962. The force also occupied the former Governor's House.

THE INTERIOR OF THE OLD PRISON
c1950 H41004

By 1818 the prison within the castle was already considered inadequate despite only having been built in 1779 and plans were drawn up for a new prison in the outer ward. It was closed in 1878 and subsequently became the headquarters of the Pembrokeshire Police. In 1967 the building was converted to house the Pembrokeshire County Museum and Records Office. The latter is still housed there today. One of the doors to these cells pictured here is on display in the Town Museum in the castle precinct.

THE CASTLE c1955 H41045

A panoramic view of the town and castle showing how the latter dominated the scene even in 1955. Note the scaffolding around the tower.

THE CASTLE

GENERAL VIEW C1950 H41002

A good view of the town centre, the castle centre-stage and the watchtower of the new prison building behind it. The tower of St Thomas's can be seen extreme left and the spire of St Martin's extreme right.

The castle was granted to Henry, Duke of Buckingham in 1483 but he was executed in the same year and it came into the ownership of Richard Williams from 1484. His was a slightly longer tenure, but as a supporter of Richard III, soon to lose all at Bosworth Field, the new Tudor dynasty conferred the ownership on Jasper Tudor. Upon his death in 1495 the title passed to one Henry, Duke of York - the future King Henry VIII. He granted it to Anne Boleyn - who held it only briefly! From this point onwards the castle was only sporadically maintained while the town continued to develop. The castle slipped into decline and by 1577 it was described as "utterlie decayed" but there was a prison there then - a "rounde tower, under which is a strong prison house".

By the time of the Civil Wars of the mid-17th century the castle was deemed incapable of being seriously defended and after the Parliamentarian victory it was slighted in 1648 (deliberately reduced so as to make it indefensible) on the orders of no other than Oliver Cromwell.

In 1777 came the publication of a report entitled 'The State of the Prisons in England and Wales' by John Howard, the Sheriff of Bedfordshire. His comments on the prison in the castle were particularly damning: "This Gaol is also the Bridewell. The two lowest rooms are very damp dungeons, in one of these a prisoner lost first the use of his limbs and then his life … The upper rooms are dirty and offensive with small windows. No sewers, no courtyard."

Following John Howard's report an Act was passed in 1779 for the building of a new gaol in the inner ward of the castle. It cost £1,200 and was completed by 1 December 1780 The same John Howard was pleased with the result on his visit in 1782 but it is clear that problems of overcrowding after this date caused much concern. There were 415 French prisoners of war held in the gaol after the abortive Fishguard invasion of 1797 and again in 1813. By 1817 it was widely felt that yet another improved gaol was required and by 1820 a spacious new gaol was built in the outer ward with 110 cells. After 1821 the authorities made use of a treadmill to occupy the prisoners in the grinding of flour (an occupation carefully chosen so as not to jeopardise any existing trades in the town). It was built in the inner ward of the castle and reached by a passage from the main gaol. The treadmill was a considerable deterrent to potential wrongdoers. There were two wheels, each five feet in diameter and the prisoners were made to work for ten hours in the summer and seven in winter turning the wheel at a rate of 48 steps per minute for 15 turns, after which five minute's rest was allowed.

Not long after the new gaol was opened there was an abortive escape attempt when a prisoner sent a letter asking to be supplied with a set of files and a saw. The gaoler intercepted the tools and later discovered a rope twisted out of rags in the man's cell and also discovered that he had used the mainspring of his watch to cut half-way through the bars. The offender was clapped in irons.

The last man hanged in the gaol was William Robin, found guilty of murder. Sentence was passed on 23 April 1821 and his execution was witnessed by a considerable crowd of townsfolk. His body was handed over to be "dissected and anatomised". In 1878 the prison was closed and the inmates transferred to Carmarthen gaol.

THE TOWN FROM THE CASTLE C1965 H41074

Looking to the north-east the course of the Western Cleddau can just be seen at the bottom of the picture beyond what would have been part of the Marychurch Foundry. The extensive car park, now redeveloped, was once part of the river (see 27945, page 19).

THE CASTLE

Above: THE CASTLE FROM THE RIVER 1890 27940

An evocative view from the north-east of the part of the town immediately below the castle and the impressive castle and prison itself. The watch-tower in the roof of the new prison was built so the guards could observe all activity in the exercise yards. These buildings in the shadow of the castle walls were the site of the Marychurch Foundry, the town's biggest employer until its closure in the mid-1930s.

Above Right: THE TOWN FROM THE RIVER 1890 27942

A superb view looking up the Western Cleddau into Haverfordwest with the castle in the centre and the tower of St Thomas à Becket on the hill overlooking it. Note the steamer in the forefront of the picture. The Priory ruins can just be seen across the river and below St Thomas's.

Opposite: SCOTCHWELL WALK 1906 53755

A veritable oasis of calm after the hustle and bustle of Haverfordwest town centre.

ALONG THE PEMBROKESHIRE COAST PATH FROM LITTLE HAVEN TO ST DAVID'S

ALONG THE PEMBROKESHIRE COAST PATH FROM LITTLE HAVEN TO ST DAVID'S

AMONGST the treasures of this part of Wales are the scenery and historic sites which can be found along the Pembrokeshire Coastal Path, within easy reach of Haverfordwest.

The craggy, steep but captivating Pembrokeshire coastline is amply demonstrated in this view (left) of

Little Haven. It is a somewhat different story in the depths of winter, when this coast is regularly battered by storms. Little Haven, at the end of a narrow valley at the foot of a steep hill, has been a popular seaside resort for many years. It also had nearby coal pits, which sent out some of their produce from the beach here.

The sandy beach of Broad Haven, on the coast of St Bride's Bay, was a fashionable bathing place in the 19th century and is still popular today. People in B469027 (page 76) are exploring in the rock pools. In the view 41100 (page 75), Star Rock is just visible below the far headland. Broad Haven is sheltered from south-westerlies by the bulk of St Bride's Peninsula.

The beach at Newgale is the longest in Pembrokeshire (two miles end to end), lying below a shingle storm ridge. The old road follows the line of the ridge and the beach was occasionally used to load coal onto boats at high tide from the nearby Trefan Cliff Colliery.

The village of Solva was in former times something of a wrecker's haven, with many of the old houses having secret cupboards and holes in which goods could be stashed away. Solva 'had the reputation of hanging out false lights to decoy the wandering mariner in order to benefit from his misfortunes' (Richard Fenton, 1811).

Lower Solva is built around the harbour, but there were also eight lime-kilns here in 1908. But the sea can be cruel as well as kind. In 1773 there was a terrible shipwreck nearby of the 'Phoebe and Peggy', a ship bound from Philadelphia to Liverpool. 60 people were drowned and the cargo lost. Seven fishing boats set out to help but one of these was also lost with all hands when it struck Black Rock.

St David's is in a somewhat austere location on its windswept plateau, but boasts the remains of an impressive bishop's palace as well as its historic cathedral. St David's, or Tyddewi, is named after Dewi Sant, the patron saint of Wales who established his monastery

Top: Little Haven, Black Rocks 1898 41100A

Above: Little Haven, The Beach 1898 41101

Strawberry Hill, above the village, was the site of an Iron Age fort. A boat is being beached to the right beyond the slipway.

here on the site of the River Alun. The legend has it that David, about to speak to an assembled crowd, was concerned they would not be able to see him. He dropped his handkerchief on to the ground, which sank down, forming a hollow, a natural amphitheatre in which everyone could see and hear him. The cathedral was later built on this spot. Another local legend tells that the wife of a heathen chief called Boia told her maids 'to go where the monks can see you with bodies bare, play games and use lewd words', in order to tempt the monks away from their vows. Dewi Sant remained strong, and thereafter he and his monks worked with heads bowed in case they should see more temptations of the world. The same legend also says that Boia and his camp were promptly all destroyed by heavenly fire! St David died on 1 March in the year AD588.

The purple sandstone for the bishop's palace was quarried from the cliffs above Caerfai Bay (S14161, page 80). Life on this peninsula was hard, for the monks as well as the local farmers: 'They place the yoke on their own shoulders; they dig into the ground with mattocks and spades, they provide with their own labour all the necessities of the community.' (From 'Life of David', c1090.)

The cathedral complex, much of which can still be seen today, was once surrounded by a curtain wall – the Norman response to its having been attacked and pillaged at least eight times! Giraldus Cambrensis (a statue of whom can be seen in the cathedral) had this to say: 'St David's is the head and in times past was the metropolitan city of Wales, though now, alas, keeping more of the name than the effect.'

BROAD HAVEN, THE BEACH 1898 41100

Broad Haven, The View from the Rocks c1960 B469027

Newgale, The Beach c1960 N64024

In 1690 the 'Resolution' was wrecked here and robbed 'by the more unmerciful people of the neighbourhood'.

ROCH, THE CASTLE c1955 R293011

The castle was built by the de la Roche family in the late 12th/early 13th centuries. It rises up dramatically from a volcanic outcrop. Legend has it that the first owner, Adam de la Roche, was told by a local witch that he would die from the bite of a snake, but if he lived (adder-free) for a year the prophecy would not come to fruition. He ordered the castle to be built on a rocky outcrop to confound the local serpents and confined himself to the tower. All seemed to be going swimmingly right up until the last day of the curse. He was cold and sent for firewood. Unfortunately, the bundle of sticks included an adder, which, of course, bit him, and Adam died. This is one of the 'Landsker' castles, which formed an early boundary between the 'Englishry' and the 'Welshry'. The tower would originally have been surrounded by a bailey wall, and outside that by a double ditch and bank. During the Civil Wars of the mid 17th century it was first held for the King by the Earl of Carberry in 1642, but surrendered to Colonel Rowland Laugharne in the February of 1644. It changed hands again in July of the same year and stayed in the Royalist camp until early 1645. The castle was converted into a private residence in 1902.

Above: NEWGALE, THE OLD WELSH ROAD 1954 N64025

A change in sea level and erosion have combined to produce a fascinating effect off this beach, as documented by Giraldus Cambrensis: 'We then passed over Niwegal sands, at which place (during the winter that King Henry II spent in Ireland), as well as in almost all other western ports, a very remarkable circumstance occurred. The sandy shores of South Wales, being laid bare by the extraordinary violence of a storm, the surface of the earth, which had been covered for many age, re-appeared, and discovered the trunks of trees cut off, standing in the very sea itself, the strokes of the hatchet appearing as if made yesterday.'

Leftt: SOLVA, MAIN ROAD c1965 S413083

There is a classic three-wheeler car on the right of this photograph.

Along the Pembrokeshire Coast Path from Little Haven to St David's

HAVERFORDWEST

Left: Solva, The Harbour c1955 S413024

When the artist Augustus John (1878-1961) passed through the area he commented: 'Solva proved so pleasant that two or three weeks passed before we took the road to St David's.

Above: Solva, From the Gribbin c1955 S413015

Along the Pembrokeshire Coast Path from Little Haven to St David's

Right: SOLVA, MIDDLE HILL C1960 S413092

Below: ST DAVID'S, CAERFAI BAY C1960 S14161

Above: ST DAVID'S, THE CATHEDRAL, THE CHOIR EAST 1890 27915

The interior of the cathedral is simply stunning. The roof beams were renewed in the 19th century. The Bishop's Throne, dating from c1500, is on the right before the open wooden screen, which separates the choir from the presbytery. The tomb beyond the screen is that of Edmund Tudor, the Earl of Richmond.

Right: ST DAVID'S, THE CATHEDRAL, THE INTERIOR c1955 S14044

ALONG THE PEMBROKESHIRE COAST PATH FROM LITTLE HAVEN TO ST DAVID'S

St David's, From the South-West
1890 27908

"*When the evening sun falls over St David's Cathedral, gilding the old stone, shining on the gentle green hills, the white twisting roads and the little farms, the smallest 'city' in the kingdom lies lost in its mighty memories. The sea wind drops, the smoke rises ...ward from the chimneys, and a man looking at the church in the hollow knows it to possess the longest memory in Britain.*"

H V Morton, 1932

ALONG THE PEMBROKESHIRE COAST PATH FROM LITTLE HAVEN TO ST DAVID'S

Left: ST DAVID'S, THE CATHEDRAL
c1960 S14130

Below: ST DAVID'S, THE CATHEDRAL,
ST MARY'S CHAPEL 1890 27920

This is in the remains of the extensive bishop's palace, which is now much restored. William the Conqueror once journeyed here to pray in this well-known place of pilgrimage. The medieval name for St David's was 'Menevia', from the Welsh 'Mynyw', which is itself derived from the Irish 'Muine', meaning a bush - hence the phrase 'Roma semel quantum bis dat Menevia tantum', which translates as 'Once to Rome is equal to twice to St David's'.

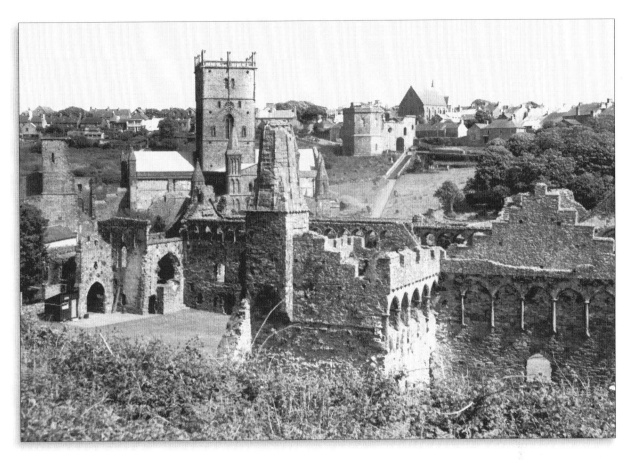

Above: ST DAVID'S,
THE CATHEDRAL AND THE BISHOP'S
PALACE C1960 S14123

The cathedral is seen across the magnificent bishop's palace built by Henry Gower. On the right is a wheel window just visible in the east gable. Note also the arcading on the top of the walls.

Right: ST DAVID'S, WHITESAND BAY
C1960 S14183

There is a chapel dedicated to St Patrick in the Bay, marked by a plaque; he is said to have set out for Ireland from here.

St David's, Cross Square c1950   S14050

Silver and lead were mined nearby in the reign of Elizabeth I (1558-1603).

Names of Subscribers

The following people have kindly supported this book by purchasing limited edition copies prior to publication.

To Terry and Laura with love from Sarah

Cam and Annie, 25/11/2005

Bob and Jenny Cole

Mr & Mrs H Cummings

Matilda Ernest, in memory of Max

Herbert Foster

Mrs & Mrs K Gilbert, Haverfordwest

Mr & Mrs J B Grimwood, of Dreenhill

To Charles and Connie Gwilliam

Mr & Mrs Len Jenkins

Dai Jones and family

Jennifer and Len Jones

Mrs & Mrs F B Jones and family

D Jones and son Robert

John Jones and family

Remembering Anthony Laplanche, Lambston

Vernon, Sue, Rob and Cheri Mansell

To celebrate the birth of Ethan Merry

John and Julia Morgan

Michael Peachey and Harry Jones

Mr & Mrs F D Pitman

Thomas Family Prendergast, Haverfordwest

Hugh Thomas Prendergast, Haverfordwest

To our son John Price on his 21st birthday, love Mum and Dad

John and Emilia Roughton

Jack Seed

James Stevenson and family

William Gwyther Thomas, 1907 - 1991. Divisional Highways Surveyor, Pembrokeshire County Council, 1945 - 1972

Bob Thomas, best wishes on your 60th

Ivor Thomas and sons John and Jeb

Mr & Mrs D A Towler, Haverfordwest

Mr & Mrs R Vickers, Portfield Gate, Haverfordwest

Mrs & Mrs D Williams

Ivor Williams and wife Maureen

Jack and Margaret Williams and family

INDEX

FRITH PRODUCTS & SERVICES

Francis Frith would doubtless be pleased to know that the pioneering publishing venture he started in 1860 still continues today. Over a hundred and forty years later, The Francis Frith Collection continues in the same innovative tradition and is now one of the foremost publishers of vintage photographs in the world. Some of the current activities include:

INTERIOR DECORATION

Today Frith's photographs can be seen framed and as giant wall murals in thousands of pubs, restaurants, hotels, banks, retail stores and other public buildings throughout the country. In every case they enhance the unique local atmosphere of the places they depict and provide reminders of gentler days in an increasingly busy and frenetic world.

PRODUCT PROMOTIONS

Frith products are used by many major companies to promote the sales of their own products or to reinforce their own history and heritage. Frith promotions have been used by Hovis bread, Courage beers, Scots Porage Oats, Colman's mustard, Cadbury's foods, Mellow Birds coffee, Dunhill pipe tobacco, Guinness, and Bulmer's Cider.

GENEALOGY AND FAMILY HISTORY

As the interest in family history and roots grows world-wide, more and more people are turning to Frith's photographs of Great Britain for images of the towns, villages and streets where their ancestors lived; and, of course, photographs of the churches and chapels where their ancestors were christened, married and buried are an essential part of every genealogy tree and family album.

FRITH PRODUCTS

All Frith photographs are available Framed or just as Mounted Prints and Posters (size 23 x 16 inches). These may be ordered from the address below. Other products available are- Address Books, Calendars, Jigsaws, Canvas Prints, Coasters, Notelets and local and prestige books.

THE INTERNET

Already ninety thousand Frith photographs can be viewed and purchased on the internet through the Frith websites and a myriad of partner sites.

For more detailed information on Frith companies and products, look at this site:
www.francisfrith.com

See the complete list of Frith Books at: www.francisfrith.com
This web site is regularly updated with the latest list of publications from The Francis Frith Collection. If you wish to buy books relating to another part of the country that your local bookshop does not stock, you may purchase on-line.

For further information, trade, or author enquiries please contact us at the address below:
The Francis Frith Collection, Frith's Barn, Teffont, Salisbury, Wiltshire, England SP3 5QP.
Tel: +44 (0)1722 716 376 Fax: +44 (0)1722 716 881 Email: sales@francisfrith.co.uk

---

See Frith products on the internet at www.francisfrith.com

FREE PRINT OF YOUR CHOICE

Mounted Print
Overall size 14 x 11 inches (355 x 280mm)

Choose any Frith photograph in this book.
Simply complete the Voucher opposite and
return it with your remittance for £3.50 (to cover
postage and handling) and we will print the
photograph of your choice in SEPIA (size 11 x 8
inches) and supply it in a cream mount with a
burgundy rule line (overall size 14 x 11 inches).
Please note: **aerial photographs and
photographs with a reference number
starting with a "Z" are not Frith photographs
and cannot be supplied under this offer.
Offer valid for delivery to one UK address only**.

**PLUS: Order additional Mounted Prints
at HALF PRICE - £9.50 each** (normally £19.00)
If you would like to order more Frith prints from
this book, possibly as gifts for friends and family,
you can buy them at half price (with no
additional postage and handling costs).

PLUS: Have your Mounted Prints framed
For an extra £18.00 per print you can have your
mounted print(s) framed in an elegant polished
wood and gilt moulding, overall size
16 x 13 inches (no additional postage and
handling required).

IMPORTANT!

**These special prices are only available if you use
this form to order. You must use the ORIGINAL
VOUCHER on this page (no copies permitted). We
can only despatch to one UK address. This offer
cannot be combined with any other offer.**

Send completed Voucher form to:
**The Francis Frith Collection, Frith's Barn,
Teffont, Salisbury, Wiltshire SP3 5QP**

CHOOSE A PHOTOGRAPH FROM THIS BOOK

Voucher for **FREE** and Reduced Price Frith Prints

*Please do not photocopy this voucher. Only the original is valid,
so please fill it in, cut it out and return it to us with your order.*

Picture ref no	Page no	Qty	Mounted @ £9.50	Framed + £18.00	Total Cost £
		1	Free of charge*	£	£
			£9.50	£	£
			£9.50	£	£
			£9.50	£	£
			£9.50	£	£
			£9.50	£	£
Please allow 28 days for delivery. Offer available to one UK address only			* Post & handling		£3.50
			Total Order Cost		£

Title of this book . . . .

I enclose a cheque/postal order for £ . . . .
made payable to 'The Francis Frith Collection'

OR please debit my Mastercard / Visa / Maestro card,
details below

Card Number:

Issue No (Maestro only):   Valid from (Maestro):

Card Security Number: Expires:

Signature:

Name Mr/Mrs/Ms . . . .

Address . . . .

. . . .

. . . .

. . . . Postcode . . . .

Daytime Tel No . . . .

Email . . . .

Valid to 31/12/12

Can you help us with information about any of the Frith photographs in this book?

We are gradually compiling an historical record for each of the photographs in the Frith archive. It is always fascinating to find out the names of the people shown in the pictures, as well as insights into the shops, buildings and other features depicted.

If you recognize anyone in the photographs in this book, or if you have information not already included in the author's caption, do let us know. We would love to hear from you, and will try to publish it in future books or articles.

An Invitation from The Francis Frith Collection to Share Your Memories

The 'Share Your Memories' feature of our website allows members of the public to add personal memories relating to the places featured in our photographs, or comment on others already added. Seeing a place from your past can rekindle forgotten or long held memories. Why not visit the website, find photographs of places you know well and add YOUR story for others to read and enjoy? We would love to hear from you!

www.francisfrith.com/memories

Our production team

Frith books are produced by a small dedicated team at offices in the converted Grade II listed 18th-century barn at Teffont near Salisbury, illustrated above. Most have worked with the Frith Collection for many years. All have in common one quality: they have a passion for the Frith Collection.

Frith Books and Gifts

We have a wide range of books and gifts available on our website utilising our photographic archive, many of which can be individually personalised.

www.francisfrith.com